charles comfort

charles comfort

canadian artists 2
margaret gray
margaret rand
lois steen

gage publishing

In October 2014
CHARLIE HILL
gave this book to
ADAM WELCH

Gage Publishing
Copyright Margaret Gray, Margaret Rand, Lois Steen, 1976

Canadian Cataloguing in Publication Data

Gray, Margaret Blair
  Charles Comfort

(Canadian art series (Agincourt, Ont.); no. 2)

  Bibliography: p. 74
  ISBN 0-7715-9988-9
  1. Comfort, Charles Fraser, 1900-
  I. Rand, Margaret, 1918-   II. Steen, Lois.
  III. Title.   IV. Series.
  ND249.C56G73   759.11   C76-017082-7

List of Illustrations

Preface

There are a number of fine Canadian artists who emerged just after the Group of Seven and who have been to a great extent overshadowed by the almost hypnotic public concentration on the spectacular Group. These artists, born within a decade of the turn of the century, are still producing today, and we believe they deserve greater recognition.

We are not attempting to make comparisons or judgments, but to acquaint Canadians with artists who have made and continue to make important contributions to our national heritage. We have visited them in their homes and these biographies are based on personal interviews. They have told us about their lives, the events and influences they consider significant, and the circumstances under which some of their works came into being. We have freely used direct quotations. How better could we express the artist's own ideas?

It is appropriate that Charles Comfort, who has a fine sense of history, should live in the historic Scott House, built on the site of the home of Philomen Wright, first citizen of Hull, Quebec. We were ushered into the high-ceilinged living room with its unique five-bay window on what must have been the hottest day of a hot summer.

But Charles Comfort remained cool and unperturbed as he answered our questions and recounted his own interesting history. His wife, Louise, rounded out his story with her own contributions. They were warm, friendly and open with us, and made our task as pleasant and easy as possible.

We have had the privilege of viewing a number of fine private collections. Many of these collectors wish to remain anonymous, but to all of them we say a very sincere thank you for their courtesy and co-operation and their permission to photograph.

A number of art galleries and institutions have also graciously given us access to their collection: National Gallery of Canada; War Museum of Canada; Art Gallery of Ontario; Art Gallery of Hamilton; London Public Library & Art Museum; Hart House, University of Toronto; Victoria University, Toronto; Toronto Stock Exchange; Ron & Ron Design Consultants, John Evans Photography, Mrs. Roland Michener. We gratefully acknowledge their courtesy and co-operation.

Margaret Gray
Margaret Rand
Lois Steen

Charles Comfort

Charles Fraser Comfort, O.C., LL.D., R.C.A. Emeritus Director of the National Gallery of Canada, is a distinguished Canadian artist. As with the men of the Renaissance this does not, however, tell the whole tale. He is also writer, teacher, lecturer, photographer, soldier, a man of wide interests and insatiable curiosity. This diversification has not diluted the strength of his greatest talent, rather it has deepened his insight and opened the windows that illuminate his art.

Comfort is a man of paradoxes: with little formal schooling, he is a highly educated man; prudent and conservative, he has made many daring and innovative moves; a private person, he was thrown into the relentless spotlight of public life as Director of the National Gallery, and the cloak of imperturbable dignity covered a warm and generous human being; a complex man, yet he has been guided throughout his life by the simple principles of honour, integrity and goodness. His life has been filled with rich and varied experiences and, like Tennyson, he is a part of all that he has met.

It is always interesting to see where and how an unusual talent first manifests itself. With Charles Comfort, the setting was a stately home in England. Although born in Scotland, young Charles was sent at the age of three to live with his grandmother who was chief laundress at Hadham Hall in Hertfordshire. It was here that he first showed his artistic tendencies. Discovering that a chunk of laundry starch could be used as chalk, he proceeded to decorate the walls and floor of the laundry with drawings. Shocked though his grandmother was, she recognized his talent and, when he later won first prize for drawing and brushwork at school, she began to consider him for the respectable career of architect (to become an artist, like becoming an actor, was not to be thought of in his strongly religious family!).

Charles has many happy memories of his childhood at Hadham Hall:

To live in a seventeenth-century mansion like that, even from a "downstairs" level (you've

"Charles in his kilt, Hadham Hall, September 1907"

seen the television programme, Upstairs, Downstairs? Well, we were "downstairs.") was a tremendous experience. I've kept in touch all these years with Miss Susan Minet, the daughter of the owner of Hadham Hall . . . and I've been back to visit several times.

But this part of his life, and his grandmother's ambitions for him, came to an end at the age of eleven when he was sent back to Scotland because his father and mother had decided to emigrate to Canada now that their family had increased to eight children.

They sailed on 6 April, 1912, aboard a small ship called the *Saturnia*. It was a nerve-racking voyage, as the boat threaded its way in the fog through iceberg-ridden seas. If exciting for the twelve-year-old Charles, for the adults aboard anxiety turned to near panic at the news that the *Titanic* had struck an iceberg and sunk in these waters. The ordeal was finally over when they steamed into the harbour of Saint John, N.B. They then travelled west by train and settled in Winnipeg.

Charles Comfort's father had a good education but no specific occupation and it was some time before he found employment in the treasury department of the City of Winnipeg. Charles, as the eldest, although not yet twelve, had to go to work immediately to help support the family. He got a job as a water-boy on an asphalt gang at a dollar a day.

In his spare time he kept up his painting, using as models whatever was to hand, and like Rembrandt, his first portraits were of his sisters. At thirteen he submitted several water colours to a YMCA competition and won first prize. This was a significant event in Charles' life because the judge was Fred Brigden, a well-known Canadian artist who had commercial studios both in Toronto and Winnipeg. He was so impressed with the boy's work that he offered him a position in his Winnipeg studio at the apprentice-wage of three dollars a week. This was a blow to the family as, with such a small weekly pay-cheque, Charles had to reduce his contribution to the household. But it was the beginning of Charles Comfort's career and he remained with Brigden's for fifteen years. Pleased at how well he could draw, Brigden's gave him a great variety of work. He drew furniture, kitchen-ware of all kinds, agricultural machinery, equipment and harness for horses. There were no colour photographs in those days and everything for colour work had to be drawn in colour and then reproduced from copper or zinc plates or wood blocks, one for each colour.

In the evenings he attended art classes first at a technical school and then at the Winnipeg School

"Charles Comfort at his drafting table
at Brigden's Ltd. Winnipeg, 1916"

of Art from which he later graduated. In the formal and structured classes he found the discipline of learning to draw from plaster casts somewhat restricting after the freehand work he did by day, but he persevered, recognizing that this discipline was necessary to gain mastery over the mechanics of his craft. From casts he moved to models and eventually to nude models at the age of eighteen. (Under eighteen, students were considered too young to be exposed to nudes.)

As he matured, other interests were developing. He discovered the joys of music; he took violin lessons, and collected records with all his spare money. In 1917 he attended his first live symphony which had a tremendous impact on him. He recalls:

> *It was on such an occasion as this that one discovered the means to best reveal the subtleties of one's inner thoughts. Did music realize these insights more readily than language or painting?*

Charles also became involved with the Winnipeg Little Theatre, designing sets and playing small parts. He worked alongside artists like Walter Phillips, and LeMoine Fitzgerald, enjoying the camaraderie and gaining useful experience. Set painting was a good introduction to the mural painting for which he would later become famous.

In 1918 and 1919 Charles Comfort won the T. Eaton Company annual country-wide competition for catalogue covers. Intrigued by the great things he had heard about Toronto, he decided to take the prize money and go there to find out for himself.

When he arrived in Toronto on 1 December, 1919, he was met at Union Station by Tom McLean, a Brigden's man he had met in Winnipeg. He stayed with the McLeans until he found a room on Jarvis Street. Tom showed him the city, introduced him to friends, and took him to the Arts & Letters Club, a club which he soon joined and of which he has been a member ever since. Here he met a number of congenial artists, all of whom were friendly and helpful.

> *The Arts & Letters Club, founded in 1908, was to become the matrix of many artistic endeavours, including the Group of Seven, the Hart House Theatre, the Hart House Quartette, and later, the Canadian Group of Painters. Its importance in the development of the arts in Canada cannot be exaggerated, nor its importance in the development of individual artists.*

Brigden's Toronto studio was pleased to have Comfort work for them while he was in the city and he became a kind of mobile employee, moving back and forth between Toronto and Winnipeg as required. He was in Toronto in May

"Charles and his brothers and sisters, Winnipeg, 1916"

1920, in time to see the first exhibition of the Group of Seven.

The first impact of the exhibition on me as a young student was one of burgeoning colour. The second was the dynamic, almost ruthless energy employed in the use of oil paint. The third was the shift in the nature of subject matter . . . the overwhelming theme was the vigorous beautiful challenge of the little-known wilderness of the north, the unconquered territory of unexplored and unclaimed natural treasure that was suddenly revealed . . . by the group who were being referred to as "rebellious young men."

His eyes wide open, he greedily took in the new impressions, the dynamic ideas. At the Arts & Letters Club he met and talked to these "rebellious young men" who were expressing the Canadian landscape in an utterly new and exciting way. They encouraged him to move out beyond his academic training and extend his own vision, showing him new possibilities for his own work rather than leaving their imprint on his style.

Charles Comfort held his first exhibition in a chartered gallery in Winnipeg in 1922. He had been a member of the Winnipeg Sketch Club for some time and Frank Johnston (at that time member of the Group of Seven) as Director of the Winnipeg Art Gallery asked Comfort if he and some of his sketching friends would put on an exhibition of about fifty paintings. In the end it was a two-man show, Charles Comfort and F. T. Moore Beatty. The anniversary of this event was celebrated fifty years later on 19 October, 1972 at the Winnipeg Art Gallery with a splendid one-man retrospective show opened by Mrs. Roland Michener, wife of the then Governor-General, and one of his earliest patrons. It was here that she described Comfort as "a modern veritable Canadian Renaissance Man."

When the show ended in the fall of 1922, Charles left Winnipeg to study at the Art Students' League in New York.

This was the beginning of possibly the most important instruction I had. It was very different from what I had had either at Tech or at the Winnipeg School of Art because you met men of rank and experience who were interested in you and in how they might change your ideas. They weren't going to interfere with how you painted so much.

His principal teacher was Robert Henri, "a very great person in his own right."

Henri would ask me if I'd ever studied Velasquez and I'd say "I'm sorry, sir, I've heard of him but I've never seen anything by Velasquez." Or was I

"Winnipeg, 1924"

*aware of the painting of El Greco, or had I seen
anything of Rubens? Well, these painters as far as
I was concerned were just names. But he would
say, "Oh, there are some good paintings by these
people right here in New York at the Metropolitan
or at the Frick, and I suggest you go and see
them."*

Comfort remembers Henri coming in one day
when he was painting and asking: "Do you
always work on a white canvas? You never lay an
imprimatura?" Charles did not know what the
term meant. Henri explained and showed him
how to lay an undercoat on his canvas using a
tone that would bring up the values of the colour
scheme he intended to use, a technique Comfort
still employs.

Another of his teachers was Euphrasius Allen
Tucker, the man who had assembled and written
the catalogue for the famous Armory Show in
1913. He introduced Comfort to the works of
Cézanne as a basis for understanding modern
art.

For two years at the Art Students' League he was
bombarded by art in all forms. His fellow
students were revolutionaries, experimenters,
refusing to be bound by the classical canons,
writing a new definition of the term "art." For a
conventional young man in his early twenties,
the experience was electrifying. While not

himself of the temperament to be a rebel, the
influences can be seen in the release of an
imaginative quality into the realism of his
painting.

At the end of the two-year period he returned to
Winnipeg and to Brigden's. He resumed his
sketching, his Little Theatre activities, his music
—and his friendship with Louise Chase, whom
he met before going to New York. Their courting
took place in Winnipeg and at her father's cottage
on Lake of the Woods. They married in 1924, the
beginning of a remarkably happy and productive
partnership in which Louise has been, for over
fifty years, wife, mother, secretary and agent.
She complements her husband, filling his needs
with encouragement and love. There have been
rough patches over the years, but there have
been many more occasions for joy and laughter.
Louise says she is content to leave to posterity the
question of her husband's greatness—but for her
there is no doubt.

The Comforts made a permanent move to
Toronto in April, 1925. In the mid-twenties and
thirties, owing largely to the activities of the Arts
& Letters Club, Toronto provided a rich and
stimulating cultural climate for a young artist.

*The community was small enough for artists,
musicians, writers, and university professors to
form an integral group of friends who worked*

PRAIRIE ROAD

Prairie Road was worked up from a sketch brought with him from Winnipeg. His first large oil, it was shown by the O.S.A. in 1925 and immediately "snapped up" by Hart House.

Collection of Hart House, University of Toronto
46″ x 34″   oil   1925

DRAWING OF LOUISE

Comfort's sensitive draftsmanship shows in this beautiful sketch of his wife in a pensive moment.

Collection of Mrs. Charles Comfort
8″ x 10″   pencil   1925

LOUISE

Here we see the brooding quality of a Rembrandt though not the technique. His sensual use of colour, the subtle use of light (behind the shoulders and head) began at this time and have continued to be his chief artistic concerns. This painting is here reproduced in colour for the first time.

Collection of Mrs. Charles Comfort
26" x 20"   oil   1927

13

together and played together, sharing philosophical discussions; reading aloud to one another the current plays and poetry; listening to contemporary music; producing and acting in amateur theatre — a never-ending source of enrichment and development.

Lawren Harris saw Charles Comfort's first large canvas, *Prairie Road*, which he had worked up from a sketch done in Winnipeg. Much impressed, Harris urged him to submit it to the Ontario Society of Artists' show in 1925. It was accepted and after the exhibition, was bought by Hart House, University of Toronto, where it hangs today.

About the same time that the Comforts arrived in Toronto, another young man, Will Ogilvie, came to work at Brigden's. Will came from South Africa with a very different background and new ideas, which Charles found most interesting. A friendship sprang up between the two men and Will was a frequent visitor at the Comforts'. Louise and her baby daughter posed for Ogilvie's *Madonna and Child* which he painted for the chapel at Hart House.

Because both men were doing a great deal of painting they decided to take a studio together on Grenville Street. It was here that Comfort produced many of his well-known works, including *Louise,* the beautiful, sensitive portrait

of his wife, and a portrait of his friend Norman Robinson, *The Dreamer.* His reputation as a fine portraitist was fast being established with works such as these, where he goes beyond mere likeness and brings out something of the essence of the sitter.

Sketching trips — like busman's holidays — were Charles Comfort's recreation. Almost always with Louise, but also frequently with other artists, he would go off for a day into the environs of Toronto or further afield for weekends. For his vacation he might go north for several weeks or take an extended trip and Haliburton and Georgian Bay were favourite haunts. One summer he and Will Ogilvie took a trip to the Rockies and spent a month at the Brewster Chalet in Yoho Park. Another year he and Harold Ayres travelled to the Maritimes. The sketches he would bring back from these trips provided the raw material for the winter's work in the studio where many of them were worked up into large canvases.

Comfort recalls an amusing anecdote about Will Ogilvie when they and a couple of other artists went up to a Dr. Spaulding's cottage at Gull Lake one winter weekend. Will went down to the lake in the bitter cold of the morning to find the water hole and get a pail of water. He came back after some considerable time. The hole was covered with snow and he had found it eventually by

HAROLD AYRES Meadowvale, Ontario
Rarely did Comfort combine figures and landscape, though he has always done each separately.
This painting is reminiscent of the light-filled early watercolours of the American, Winslow Homer.

Collection of Dr. S. Demeter   9″ x 10″   w.c.   1925

GULL LAKE (Near Minden)
In this early water colour there is
a tentative, subtle interaction of
colour. Compare this gentle
beginning with his later strong
landscapes in oil.

Collection of Dr. Steven Demeter
10" x 9"   w.c.   undated

16

falling into the icy water from which he emerged with his clothes frozen stiff. The story went the rounds with Will's comments about the rigours of the Canadian climate compared to the temperate conditions in South Africa. The sequel came ten years later when Comfort went into a barber shop in Toronto.

> The barber asked me where I was going for my holidays and when I told him Gull Lake he said: "Did you ever hear the story about the crazy dentist who had a cottage up there? He used to paint and people who painted —you know, artists —went up with him . . . One time they went up in the winter time and they took an African with them. In the morning the African went out to get a pail of water. He found the water hole all right, but he disappeared into it and they never saw him again!" I never said a word, but I thought: "That's how legends and myths originate."

In 1926 Harold and Elizabeth Ayres joined the Comforts on a trip to Quebec City and Ile d'Orleans. Unexpectedly they met artist C. W. Jeffereys and his wife, who took them to tea with Horatio Walker, elder statesman of Canadian painting, whose canvases were fetching $15,000 on the American market.

At the Arts & Letters Club Charles also met Dr. James MacCallum, who introduced him to Georgian Bay, which was to become one of his favourite returning-places. On their first trip they arrived in the evening and as the lamps were lit in the cottage, the most marvelous paintings were revealed on the walls, murals painted by J. E. H. MacDonald, Tom Thomson, Arthur Lismer. (The paintings were later carefully removed from the walls and are presently housed in the National Gallery.) The next morning he explored the island with growing excitement as he realized that here in the early days, members of the Group of Seven had come sketching. This was the place where A. Y. Jackson had painted his famous *Terre Sauvage* and Varley his *Stormy Weather, Georgian Bay.*

Seven years after the first Group of Seven show rocked Toronto, the city came in for another shock, an exhibition by the *Société Anonyme*, in 1927. A young woman called Katherine Dreier who had been deeply impressed by the Armory Show, decided to collect and circulate throughout America an exhibition of contemporary European and American painting — such artists as Kandinsky, Picabia, Stella, Miro, representing constructivism, surrealism, abstraction. Comfort, who had been shock-proofed at the Art Students' League, was a docent (guide-lecturer) for this startling show, and this sharpened his own appreciation of innovative art.

It had a great fascination for everyone who witnessed it, though on the whole I think the Canadian public was baffled by the exhibition . . . Such of my friends as Bertram Brooker, Edna Tacon, Gordon Webber and Lawren Harris were, of course, aware and interested in the directions in which the exhibition pointed. Personally, I believe that the beginning of abstract painting in Canada, certainly in Toronto, can be dated from that period. The awakening in Montreal had to await the home-coming of Alfred Pellan . . . His exhibition in 1940 was the beginning of the great development in French Canada.

Stimulated by this show, Comfort began himself to experiment in abstract expressionism. It may surprise people to know that he continues to paint abstracts, and fine ones. He does it for his own interest and few have been publicly shown, but this is an example of Charles Comfort's flexibility in style and attitude.

The storm clouds of the Depression were gathering in the summer of 1929 but most people were happily oblivious. Rapid, Grip & Batten, Ltd. approached Comfort with such an attractive offer that he reluctantly said goodbye to Bridgen's after an association of fifteen years. Rapid, Grip & Batten had a number of special jobs for him and he signed a two-year contract at a salary almost double what he had been making.

Because all that Charles Comfort does is so carefully executed, one would assume that he works slowly. But his friend Alan Collier tells of Charles' first morning working with his new company when he was given a rush job to be ready by noon. Instead of starting to work immediately, he walked around the office meeting and chatting with his new colleagues. Then, an hour before the deadline he went into his office and produced a layout that showed a fully worked-out idea, ready on time and acceptable to the client.

When the Crash came, Charles was spared the full impact because of his contract. But Rapid, Grip & Batten were having their problems, since many of their projected jobs were cancelled or modified, and at the end of the two years they had to let Comfort go.

Unlike thousands of others who found themselves "let out" in 1931, he did not join the ranks of the unemployed. Will Ogilvie, Harold Ayres and Charles Comfort combined their considerable talents and set up a commercial studio on Bay Street in Toronto. In spite of hard times, there was a lot of work coming in, and in about a year they were able to move to better premises at 9 Adelaide Street East, above the old Ellen Bradley Restaurant. This location became a convenient place for friends from the Arts & Letters Club and the Writers' Club (of which

CAPTAIN
VANCOUVER

19

Comfort was also a member) to drop in. Coffee would be sent up from Bradley's and many lively informal discussions took place within these walls.

A number of his friends were radicals. Although Comfort did not consider himself one, he did share the feeling that perhaps some form of socialism might solve the problems of the Depression.

I travelled once on a train from Saskatoon with Mr. J. S. Woodsworth [founder of the C.C.F. party] and had a long conversation with him . . . He was a most reasonable and thinking man.

At this time he painted the portrait of Carl Schaefer, *Young Canadian*, expressing with its disillusioned eyes and empty hanging hands the isolation and despair of so many young men defeated by the Depression. This haunting water-colour portrait is said to have been shown in more galleries than any other painting in Canada.

The "Renaissance Man" prepared to accept a new challenge when, in 1932, he was commissioned to paint his first big mural for the foyer of the North American Life Assurance Company building. It was to be a huge painting, 24 feet high by about 12 feet across. Its size presented a problem, as it was much too large for the Adelaide Street studio. After some searching Comfort found a big old warehouse on Wellington Street. It was in appalling condition but it would accommodate the mural. He had a scaffolding built with a bridge which could be raised to several levels.

It was a lot of hard work. I got Carl Schaefer to help me . . . and a young student from the College of Art. It was a long hot summer. . . .

The North American Life building has now been torn down and the mural has vanished.

Not so the Toronto Stock Exchange Building, hailed when it was built in 1936-37 as the latest word in efficiency and still housing the heart-beat of Toronto's business world. Charles Comfort was commissioned not only to paint eight murals, four at each end of the trading floor, but also to design a seventy-six-foot frieze for the front of the building.

Art critic Robert Ayre, writing in the *Montreal Gazette* on 24 April, 1937, says of the frieze: "There is nothing like it in Canada," and he considers the murals the first in Canada worth travelling a distance to see. (His only exception to this sweeping statement is Will Ogilvie's decoration of the chapel in Hart House.) He further writes:

They [the architects] made no mistake in engaging Charles Comfort to do the work. One of the most individual of the younger Canadians, he combines a subtle appreciation of the true values of painting and an admirable integrity to them — it would never occur to him to allow anything shoddy to leave his hands — with a robust and daring imagination and a very practical sense of the world around him.

The building was considered daringly modern, the design for the frieze "dynamically contemporary" with its "highly stylized figures of men moving in a procession — laborers and white-collar workers, farmers, miners, travelling salesmen, bankers, scientists and so on."

Someone writing in the *Toronto Daily Star* twenty years later noted that the top-hatted stockbroker appears to be dipping into the pocket of the miner in front of him—"the oldest joke on Bay Street." The article went on to state that both the stone-mason and the artist were now dead—in Comfort's case "an exaggerated report", as Mark Twain remarked when he read his own obituary!

The historical mural *Captain Vancouver*, commissioned by the C.N.R. for the Hotel Vancouver, required months of research in exploring and working out a suitable theme.

Comfort decided upon a hypothetical occasion which could well have happened — a Potlatch given by an Indian Chief in honour of Captain Vancouver. He carefully read about the historical background, investigated the dress of the period, studied the Indian customs and artifacts, and consulted anthropologists Dr. Marius Barbeau and Dr. Douglas Leachman.

The technical problems of grouping the figures in a vertical space were pondered by the artist, and he devised an ingenious solution. Captain Vancouver, the main protagonist, stands frontally at the top of the painting, flanked by his seamen. He looks down at the Chief who is seen from the back, seated on his ceremonial chair, his arms raised in greeting. His two warriors, splendid virile Indians, are placed slightly below him in the foreground. Every detail is authentic: the pattern of the Chilkat blanket worn by the Chief, the head-dresses and ceremonial rattles of the two warriors, the uniforms of Captain Vancouver and his two sailors.

For almost thirty years the painting hung in the foyer of the Hotel Vancouver where it was much admired until, in 1969, the hotel was renovated. Mrs. Roland Michener, who had a special interest in the mural since she had watched Charles Comfort working on it when they were neighbours in Rosedale, always went to see it when she was in Vancouver. On one occasion when visiting the city with her husband, the Governor-General of Canada, she went to the hotel and found that her favourite mural had not only disappeared but that no one knew what had happened to it. She made it her business to find out. Eventually the mural was located, stored in the attic of the Vancouver manager of the Janin Construction Company which had carried out the renovation.

Mrs. Michener felt keenly that this mural, a part of our national heritage, paid for by the people of Canada, should be hung in a suitable and permanent location. Eventually the president of the construction company in Montreal gave it to her so that she could find an appropriate place for it. She decided to offer it to the University of British Columbia, of which she is a graduate. The gift was enthusiastically accepted by President Gage and his Committee on University Art.

The painting had suffered from having been rolled for storage paint-side in and the paint was cracked and peeling. Charles Comfort travelled to Vancouver where he painstakingly reworked the mural to restore it to its original state. He would accept no fee for his labours.

Plans had already been made for the official presentation when a newspaper reporter brought in a group of Indians to see the painting while it was being restored. The reporter carefully pointed out that the native people were being "put down," since they were sitting at the bottom of the mural while Captain Vancouver was standing above them.

In 1935, just three years before he painted the Captain Vancouver mural, a new facet of the "Renaissance Man" made its appearance — the teacher. Continuously until 1960 (except for his active-service war years) this man who had researched and taught himself when formal training was unavailable, now passed on his unique knowledge and experience to young aspiring artists. His teaching began at the Ontario College of Art when the principal, Fred Haines, asked him to give three classes a week in drawing. Later he introduced a course in mural painting which included slide lectures, and examination of murals in Toronto and then actual experience painting a mural on scaffolding. This course had never been offered before, nor has it been available since Comfort left the College.

Charles Comfort was appointed to the Faculty of the Department of Art and Archaeology at the University of Toronto in 1938. With the head of the Department, he designed a syllabus for a "practice course" on the *Historical Techniques of Painting.*

The course provided a good higher training in the systematic use of observation, and in value

LAKE SUPERIOR VILLAGE

Cold sunlight illumines an austere, symbolic town. The shadows are as surrealist as the toy block houses with their empty staring black eyes. Neither washing on a line nor faint smoke can conjure up people for this empty town. The composition is essentially horizontal but depth and cohesion are achieved by the grid of dark and light shapes. The importance of the railway is emphasized by the strong ribbon of track in the foreground from which the viewer looks down and over the village, while in the background bare poles fasten down the lake. With this painting Comfort won an International Award in 1938, which marked a turning point in his life, for shortly thereafter he was offered a teaching post at the University of Toronto.

Art Gallery of Ontario
Gift from the Fund of the T. Eaton Co. Ltd. for Canadian Works of Art, 1950   42" x 70"   oil   1937

BALLERINA RESTING

A ballet costume, like an academic gown, is not worn frivolously. Each symbolizes a lengthy toll of discipline and study. By stressing the bare surroundings, the plain wooden chair, the exhaustion of the dancer, the artist has given this portrait a poignant significance.

Collection of Norah Michener   30″ x 32″   w.c.   1937

24

HEINTZMAN HOUSE
This house, standing firm against the encroaching trees, is a further example of Comfort's interest in depicting symbolic endurance.

Collection of Dr. Steven Demeter   31″ x 32″   w.c.   1936

PIONEER SURVIVAL

This dark, foreboding scene is dominated by stumps (foreground), terrible natural obstacles for the pioneers who had to clear the land in order to survive and put down their own roots. Powerful, relentless nature here dwarfs the people, but Comfort has placed a spot of red for passion, for tenacity, for survival. This painting was his Diploma Deposit, admitting him to membership in the Royal Canadian Academy in 1938.

The National Gallery of Canada   40¹/₄″ x 48″   oil   1938

EMANUEL HAHN
Private Collection   26″ x 30″   w.c.   1938

judgments, both broadly human and specifically aesthetic. Our aim was toward knowledgeable appreciation and criticism rather than skilled practice, understanding by doing rather than performance as a vocation.

It began with fundamentals of design — form, space, line, colour and light—through which the student learned to analyse a painting and then to produce a composition of his own, demonstrating these fundamentals. Later the concentration was on the material techniques of painting throughout history, again with practical projects employing the different techniques. Finally, modern developments and methods were studied and again each student tried his hand at Impressionism, Cubism, Futurism, de Stijl and Abstract Expressionism.

Having attended College Art Association meetings annually over many years, I found that the Toronto course in my time was unique. To my knowledge, no college or university in the United States or Canada had a practice course anything like the one I was directing in Toronto.

A militant group at the University took up the cause and the matter flared up into a hot racist issue. There were threats of demonstrations should the painting be hung. Some members of the faculty, afraid of trouble, felt that the hanging should be at least postponed, but others believed that the University could not compromise its principles and must take a stand for artistic and moral integrity. Mrs. Michener announced her willingness to stand up to this attempted intimidation and make the presentation as scheduled. But the President, after consultation with a few members of the board, decided to yield to the vociferous minority and postponed the hanging indefinitely.

At this point, Mrs. Michener asked that the mural be hung within one month, with or without ceremony, or else be returned to her. The President accepted this solution to his dilemma and it was arranged that the painting be sent back.

The story, however, has a happy ending, and the west coast's loss is the east coast's gain. In January 1973, Mrs. Michener accompanied her husband to Charlottetown to attend the Prince Edward Island Centennial celebrations. While dancing with the Premier of the Province at the Centennial Ball, she told him about the mural. He showed an immediate and enthusiastic interest, and arranged a meeting with the Director of the Art Gallery the following morning. The Premier and the Director were able to persuade her that here the mural would find a suitable and honoured home. In April 1973, at the request of Mrs. Michener, Charles Comfort made the formal presentation and the mural hangs today in the new Confederation Library in Charlottetown.

Many brilliant artists, curators and art historians graduated from this course—Ronald Bloore, Jean Sutherland Boggs, Roloff Beny, Russell Harper and William Withrow, to name but a few.

The Comfort-Ogilvie-Ayres partnership had broken up in 1936 when Will left for Montreal to teach in the Art Association School. Comfort took Studio #5 in the Studio Building. His neighbour in #6 was A. Y. Jackson.

Alec was one of my closest friends. For years we went sketching together. We used to go up to an island in Georgian Bay . . . Alec and I used to paddle and boat our way around and go ashore somewhere and find a place to paint. It didn't take long. Everything was attractive and agreeable.

Alec would plunk himself down on a rock and begin painting immediately. Charles would carefully select his spot, set up his camp stool and umbrella, make himself completely comfortable and then open his paint box and lay out his palette. They paid no attention to each other until they had both finished.

In the summer of 1937 the Comforts took a trip to Rossport on the north shore of Lake Superior. Charles came home with sketches which he developed into the painting *Lake Superior Village.* He entered this in the Great Lakes Exhibition in 1938 which was organized by the Albright Gallery in Buffalo for American and Canadian artists from cities bordering the Great Lakes. It was a young Canadian painter who won the first prize — Charles Fraser Comfort. This was an occasion for jubilation and the Micheners gave a big party to celebrate not only the honour but the prize money — five hundred dollars was a substantial sum in 1938. "It was a lifesaver!" recalls Mrs. Comfort.

The Studio Building was located near the Micheners' home in Rosedale and Mrs. Michener often came in to watch Charles at work. She tells of the time when he was painting two water colours of ballerinas:

I really did want them very much indeed, but they were beyond my means. I always remember the day on which Charles telephoned me and told me excitedly that he had just sold the Ballet Girl Seated to Gerald Larkin and that, if I came to the studio at once, I could have Ballet Girl Resting for whatever I felt I could afford to pay. This was typical of Charles' generosity.

By 1939 Charles Comfort had gained an international reputation. He had exhibited in Chicago, Buffalo, Cleveland, Detroit, Toledo, Rochester, New York and Milwaukee. In the United Kingdom his paintings had been hung in the prestigious Tate Gallery in London and in the

National Gallery in Edinburgh in his native Scotland.

His first opportunity to travel abroad came in 1939 and he sailed for Italy in May. Because of his years of reading, looking, studying, he approached the treasures of Europe with a mind cultivated and prepared, an eye trained to observe. In the great art centres of Italy he saw for the first time painting, architecture, sculpture with which he had become familiar through reproductions — a connoisseur's feast for his educated palate. In Geneva he was fortunate to see the contents of the Prado, (Madrid) which, because of the Spanish Civil War had been removed to Switzerland for safekeeping. Finally he visited Paris and the Louvre. Only later did he realize the extent of his good fortune because this was the last summer before World War II would put an end to such travel for six years, by which time some of the treasures he had enjoyed would be irrevocably lost.

As soon as war was declared, Comfort joined the Canadian Officers Training Corps at the University of Toronto and, while still teaching, was commissioned and promoted to the rank of Captain as an infantry rifle instructor.

In spite of the war, the Kingston Conference, an event important to Canadian art, took place in 1941. Sponsored by Queen's University, the National Gallery and the Carnegie Foundation, it provided an opportunity for artists from all over Canada to come to a conference at Queen's, expenses paid, and meet to discuss "The condition of art in democratic society and how it could be improved."

It was of particular interest to Charles Comfort because specialists from the Fogg Museum in Cambridge, Mass. held workshops on the chemistry of painting, discussing supports (the material which forms the surface to which the medium is applied, e.g. canvas) mediums and the nature of pigments, the subject on which he was doing his own research. It was a significant conference and out of it grew the Federation of Canadian Artists.

Early in the war, Charles Comfort and A. Y. Jackson were asked to recommend names to a committee set up to form a war art programme.

It was very difficult because we didn't know if a man would be willing to enlist on the basis of a lieutenant's pay, which was extremely small. I didn't put my name down on the first list . . . "But," they said, "We don't see your name." So my name went down. I was called up because I was already commissioned — captain's rank. But your commission papers just show where you start, as a second lieutenant. So all they need do if

ORTONA,
ITALY, 1944

PIAZZA SAN FRANCESCO DI ASSISSI Ortona
The war has exploded over this Italian village and rolled on, leaving ruin and deprivation for the survivors.
The scene is quiet after the storm but there is no sun, only a dreadful apathy.

The Canadian War Museum
The National Museum of Man
National Museums of Canada   14$^1/_2$″ x 21$^1/_2$″   w.c.   War Records 1939-45

you've got a militia commission is just give you a phone call and say, "Report to Stanley Barracks." Well, that's what happened to me . . . It's a little embarrassing walking around the streets as a 43-year-old lieutenant, when lieutenants are usually 20 or 21. Twenty-two was getting a little old!

He was sent overseas almost immediately, spent a short time in England, making a number of sketches on the south and east coast before he was sent to Italy where he made hundreds of sketches of the Italian Campaign. Near the end of the war, he was sent to Germany and northwestern Europe, then back to England. In all, he made nearly two hundred sketches from which in London, and later back in Canada, he made projections for large canvases. One of his most difficult assignments was making a painting of the Dieppe Raid which he had not witnessed and which he had to reconstruct from photographs.

Comfort has written about his experiences in the Italian Campaign in his book, *Artist at War*. He is modest about his role in the war, but it is obvious that, to do his job, an artist had to be where the action was. In addition, Comfort had been trained as a militia officer in the C.O.T.C. and on a number of occasions had to assume military duties. His friend W. E. C. Harrison, who was with him in Italy, has written an introduction to *Artist at War*. He pays tribute to the combination of genius, courage and endurance he witnessed in this artist in the field. He then refers to "this ambidextrous man, brush in one hand, pen in the other."

The pen hand has been employed as continuously as the brush hand, but not as publicly. It has contributed to scholarly journals and periodicals, to a Royal Commission study on Canadian painting and *Artist at War*. For the pleasure of his friends he has also had published privately a number of slim volumes, his "observations," his poetical impressions of places, people, events. All his life Charles Comfort has kept diaries (he filled seven during his overseas service), notes, observations and photographs (seventeen to eighteen thousand, cross-indexed), records of his experiences, reactions, impressions. This is an incredibly complete archive which one would hope will eventually become part of the National Archives — a historical document of his times, as well as his life.

Gradually the world returned to normal. The pleasant tenor of academic life had a great attraction as Comfort took up once more his role of teacher at the University. Family life resumed, painting holidays, weekend sketching trips — the blessed ordinariness that seemed so extraordinary after the dislocations of war.

In Toronto this feeling of contentment, this delight in the normal, pervaded the art scene. There was no stir of excitement such as was being sparked in Montreal by a group of young French-Canadian rebels inspired by Emile Borduas who called themselves the Automatistes. Their manifesto, the *Refus Global,* 1948, was a cry for personal liberation of the artists and individual involvement in "politics, personal security and joyful fulfilment." It immediately spawned the anti-Automatistes, led by Alfred Pellan and called the *Prisme d'Yeux.* Theirs was a demand for total liberation with no outside involvement, no responsibility to anything but their art, painting free from all bonds.

The turmoil in Montreal gave an impetus to the whole Canadian art world and in 1953 the Painters Eleven began a stormy eight-year assault on the stuffy art scene in Toronto. Exuberance and flamboyance marked the Painters Eleven and their experimental abstracts shocked Toronto. Charles Comfort at the University of Toronto observed and helped his students to analyse and understand this new movement, but was not himself involved.

In 1955 Comfort took a year off from the University when he was awarded a Royal Society Fellowship to study in Holland. His intention was to produce a bibliographic report of writings dealing with oil-painting techniques as practised by master painters in the the Netherlands. He covered the period from the fifteenth to the seventeenth century. For the first time in his life he was able to devote himself entirely to pure research, exciting and gratifying to a man who was a natural scholar. He worked with professors and specialists in Utrecht, Amsterdam and Brussels during a profitable and interesting year.

Two Netherlandish painters attracted Comfort particularly. One was Geertgen tot Sint Jans, a fifteenth-century primitive who was one of the earliest painters to experiment with the dramatic use of light. The other was the twentieth-century painter Piet Mondrian who, just before World War I,

> *. . . began to exclude everything from his art that interfered with the absolute purity of his image . . . this finally resulted in almost an architectural form of abstraction . . . There was something about that that I admired.*

By the end of the fifties, Comfort had accumulated an imposing list of honours, awards and memberships in distinguished societies. When he was awarded an honourary degree from Mount Allison University in 1958, he learned in casual conversation with a friend the

PINE ROOT Algonquin Park
The artist came upon this scene at Gilmore's Creek, Cedar Lake, Algonquin Park. This painting has a primeval feeling—a tension contained in an impressive matrix of balance and counterbalance, object and reflection, and haunting stillness.

Collection of Dr. Steven Demeter   15" x 22"   w.c.   1947

STONEHENGE II
The artist's use of back-lighting emphasizes the monumentality of these ancient slabs of stone while greatly enhancing their mystery. Jacob Bronowski suggests that "a work of art says something universal, yet something different to everyone who sees it."

Private Collection   12″ x 16″   oil   1959

36

night before the ceremony that he was expected to give the Convocation Address the next day. No one had informed him, but he got to work that night, wrote his speech and was able to carry off the affair successfully at the appointed time.

Charles was a delegate in 1959 to a NATO Conference in London at which a resolution was presented for the establishment of the Atlantic Congress, a cultural facility whereby scholars of any discipline — medicine, mathematics, painting, architecture — could move freely from one NATO country to another for their studies. The Canadian delegation was particularly interested in supporting this and it was the only resolution that was passed at this conference.

After the conference was over, Dr. and Mrs. Comfort hired a Morris Minor and set off on a painting holiday. They went first to Stonehenge, then to Bath, then up through Wales, Northern England, Scotland, following three themes: Stone Circles, the Roman Wall and Edward's Castles. They enjoyed every minute and "came home with quite a bagful of stuff."

They sailed back across the Atlantic, landing in Montreal where they picked up their car. While driving home to Toronto, Louise, who was at the wheel, had to run off the road to avoid being hit by an oncoming car which had swerved into her lane. The car skidded, went into the ditch and turned over. Louise was pinned underneath. She was very seriously hurt and it was not known if she would survive.

In his little book *Journey 1924-1964*, a tribute to Louise on the occasion of their fortieth anniversary, Charles writes of his feelings at this moment of crisis:

> *While Louise fought for her life in hospital, I lay sleepless in a hot little hotel room . . . recalling an unforgettable sequence of devoted acts of kindness and affection . . . But we have been given a reprieve—"a dividend" Louise says—"an extension."*

It was several years before she was able to walk again.

When the danger period was past, Charles returned to Toronto to prepare for his new term at the University. It was then that he heard of Alan Jarvis' resignation as Director of the National Gallery. It was not until some time later that he learned the full story.

Jarvis as Director was offered two important paintings: a Breughel (and Breughels almost never come on the market) and a Lorenzo Monaco, the fifteenth-century Italian who originated the International Style. The price for the two was less than half a million dollars, a reasonable price in 1959 and considered almost nothing in art circles today. According to Comfort, "It was a priceless opportunity. Any director with his head screwed on would have wanted to buy."

Jarvis accepted the offer. But it was just at the time of the change in government when John Diefenbaker had his landslide victory. The new Finance Minister refused to advance the money. This put Alan Jarvis in an impossible position and he resigned as Director of the National Gallery.

When the position became vacant, Comfort had a call from Ottawa asking him to apply. He talked it over with Louise who said: "No thank you!" He enjoyed his work at the University, a job without great pressures. The National Gallery position would be twenty-four hours a day, fifty-two weeks a year. However, it would be a challenge. He decided to apply. As with all Civil Service positions, it was an open competition and there were fourteen applicants. Comfort was selected. "It was the final compliment paid me."

It was indeed a challenge. Comfort inherited the groundswell of the Jarvis affair, the internal factionalism, the external damage to Canada's international reputation in the art world. The Gallery was also in the throes of moving to new quarters in the Lorne Building, not an easy time to take over.

At the age of sixty, the "Renaissance Man" had to find within himself the administrator. He had little experience in handling personnel but he pulled his department together and managed it with his characteristic efficiency. With the title of Director of the National Gallery, the top administrative post in Canada's art world, one might expect a certain self-importance. But to Comfort it was the position that was important and his responsibility to the position and the country. With his own sense of the fitness of things, he conducted himself with great dignity. In the lonely vulnerability of the office his only protection from the slings and arrows was that cloak of dignity. "Sir Charles" his staff called him, but with a fondness that would have surprised his critics.

There were many interesting opportunities for him to represent Canada at international art events and he played host to a number of distinguished representatives of other countries. He once had the somewhat sticky privilege of conducting the Queen around an exhibition of modern art which she obviously found somewhat less than admirable.

The most difficult situation he had to cope with was the Chrysler crisis. The National Gallery arranged to schedule an exhibition selected by Walter Chrysler, a well-known American collector, from his own extensive collection and

MURAL PAINTING, NATIONAL LIBRARY, OTTAWA

called *The Controversial Century.* Shortly before the date of the opening in Canada, and while the exhibition was still being shown in the U.S., a group of Americans spread the word that there were fakes in the show.

The problem did present an acute dilemma. To repudiate our agreement on the strength of a rumour would place the onus on the National Gallery and the Government of Canada to prove that the paintings were . . . fakes. And with the memory of the repudiated agreement in the case of the Breughel-Monaco purchase still very green in our minds and the resultant unfavourable publicity for Canada, it seemed particularly desirable to avoid repudiation of our agreement with Mr. Chrysler if possible. The alternative was to accept the exhibition as the personal collection of a reputable individual, as we were bound by agreement to do.

This seemed the only logical course. The show came to the National Gallery and was enjoyed by thousands of people.

A member of the National Gallery staff, for reasons best known to himself, tendered his resignation over the affair. This was an internal matter and should have remained such. But his letter of resignation was somehow released to the press. An Opposition Member brought up the matter in Parliament and demanded Comfort's resignation.

Comfort stood his ground. The trustees of the National Gallery passed a Resolution: " . . . to express their complete confidence in the administration of the Gallery under the Direction of Dr. Charles F. Comfort, and affirm their faith in the professional integrity of Dr. Comfort . . . " Unfortunately the exoneration received none of the publicity of the accusation.

Dr. Comfort continued to fulfil his duties according to his own high standards of integrity (which would not, for example, permit him to exhibit or sell his own works while he was Director of the Gallery). As in any public office, almost every decision or action drew criticism from some faction. But there were also honours, praise and endorsements. Under his directorship the Gallery established itself in its new quarters, the National Conservation Research Laboratory came into being and a number of important works of art were acquired. It was a life full of interesting and exciting encounters, a challenge well worth the cost. At the end of his five-year term, in 1965, a stimulating, if exhausting, phase of his life came to an end.

To Charles Comfort at the age of 65 it was a beginning rather than an end. For the first time in his life, and at a time when most men are retiring from active life, he became a full-time painter.

10ᵗʰ January 1963

"Charles Comfort, Director National Gallery with Governor General Georges Vanier, 1963"

In 1966 he accepted the commission to paint two murals for the reading room of the new National Library and Archives Building. They each measure 35 feet by 9 feet and took months of research. There is a Canadian wall titled *Legacy*, showing literary figures in Canadian history, and a European wall titled *Heritage*, depicting the literary giants from whom our culture is derived. The actual painting was done *in situ*, on scaffolding. Physically a most arduous task, it was executed with the skill and dexterity associated with a much younger man.

He then undertook another mural for the Academy of Medicine in Toronto, at which time the Academy made him an honourary Fellow. This same year, 1967, he was awarded the Centennial Medal. In 1972 he was honoured with Canada's highest distinction when he was made an Officer of the Order of Canada.

In the decade since he "retired," Comfort has painted innumerable landscapes which demonstrate his vitality and readiness to experiment. He is not merely repeating himself, but striking out in new directions with vigour and freedom. In this period he has also completed sixteen official portraits and is presently working on two more. Of himself and his work, Charles Comfort says:

> *I think in my own way that I am a humanist and a realist. My painting is characterized by technical conservatism — a category which has not been altogether popular in the past few years, particularly in the fifties and sixties. Yet I feel that the only valid approach to an indiginous expression is in the visual art which comes from humanistic realism.*

For Charles and Louise Comfort their partnership of more than half a century has been mutually fulfilling. Charles has gained immeasurably from his wife. Her presence has provided the climate for him to grow to his full potential. As for Louise, she wrote her feelings in the preface of Comfort's book *The Moro River and Other Observations:*

> *I have never ceased to count my blessings and to value, and enjoy to the full, the amazing qualities of my mate. For him all experience and learning . . . becomes part of a great and colourful mosaic, all of it fitting together in a remarkable and wonderful pattern of interlocking interests, all of it to be savoured again through a capturing in paint and words.*

PINES NEAR GO HOME

This is more intimate than the usual Georgian Bay paintings. It is like catching a glimpse of a secret garden.
The viewer on a slight rise looks through the dark foreground screen of trees down to a sunlit island.

Collection of G. E. Eastman   12″ x 16″   oil   1950

BATON DE HERACHES
Private Collection   23³/₄″ x 31³/₄″ x 31³/₄″   oil   1965

44

PEEP HOLE TREE
National Museums of Canada
Private Collection   12″ x 16″   oil   1963

MIDDAY, PINE ISLANDS Georgian Bay
This painting has the spectacular colour impact of Maxfield Parrish and the fanciful design of art nouveau.

Collection of Dr. Steven Demeter   24″ x 32″   oil   1966

NORTHERN SUNSET
Recently Comfort has painted several works using intense tones of one main colour—deep blue, red. This painting strongly resembles the design of Tom Thomson's "Jack Pine."

Private Collection   24″ x 32″   oil   1968

Methods and Effects

Murals and Friezes

Working with L. L. Fitzgerald and Walter Phillips on set designs for the Winnipeg Little Theatre undoubtedly gave Charles Comfort ideas and skills which he stored away until his first commissioned mural. Between 1932, when he created a mural for the North American Life Assurance Co. in Toronto (since destroyed with the building) and 1966, he painted more public murals than any other Canadian. In describing the technique he used in the National Library and Archives building in Ottawa where in 1966 he painted a mural on each wall of the Library's Reading Room, he said:

First the idea: I wished to show literary figures who had influenced the development of literature in Canada; one wall from beyond Canada, one wall from within.

From drawings made in his studio, enlargements were produced on brown paper to the scale of the wall. He then perforated the design onto the paper and pounced it down onto the canvas with a chalk bag — a 15th century method of transferring a design to a wall.

Then the action: I did the painting in situ. I had the canvas put on the wall. It was not a case where you paint in your studio and then have it marouflaged to the wall. (Marouflaging is a technique of adhesing canvas to prepared plaster wall.) I did the actual oil painting from scaffolding and with one assistant to fetch and carry. I was there the better part of six or seven months, but in all it took nearly a year longer than that from the beginning to the completion of the research. I started painting while the building was under construction around me — in fact before there were any windows in the library, and I was required to wear a hard hat.

HIS EXCELLENCY, THE RT. HON. ROLAND MICHENER

When Comfort was working on the Governor General's portrait, the often-wet canvas was transported back and forth from Scott House (Comfort's home and studio) where a clothed and be-medaled dummy, all "lace and sheep's gut" posed, to Rideau Hall where the face and hands had to be modeled from life whenever the Governor General could spare a few moments. In the three-quarter length figure, Comfort has exaggerated the angular ruggedness of the Governor General's profile with a broad, sculptural application of high colour, more impressionistic than in his usual portraits. In the background is the official crest of his high office.

Government House, Ottawa
50" x 36"   oil   1971

For the new Toronto Stock Exchange building in 1937, Comfort designed the ornamental frieze running across the entire front of the building. He actually carved a section of the one-inch-deep stone relief because "a stone mason has to know how deep to make an incision and I wanted the background bush-hammered." — (A bush hammer has a lot of small modules on it which pockmark the stone so that it catches dirt, making a dark uneven background for the figures and emphasizing the depth.)

Inside he decorated eight panels, 16 feet by 4 feet, on the end walls of the Trading Floor. One wall depicts major industries whose stocks are traded on the floor, the other represents commerce. Before he started work, Comfort spent a long time viewing the actual operations of the various industries, and then filled the panels with figures and equipment reminiscent of the powerful Depression-era murals by the great Mexican painters Rivera and Orozco. Though considered startlingly modern for their time, the stylized Stock Exchange murals were accurate in every detail.

Photography
Because photography is so universally accepted today as a recording device to catch a passing scene or some elusive light or design, as an adjunct to painting, it is interesting to have Comfort's comments:

We're living in a modern era. It is no more a sin than to use a tape recorder. I don't use photography myself in faces or hands or composition . . . I don't use it in landscape at all.

But he finds it useful in fixing drapery folds of a sitter. Of his present commissioned portrait of Dr. George Ignatieff, Provost of Trinity College, University of Toronto, he says, "I'm going to have in the background a part of Trinity College, maybe a silhouette. I use a photograph on that."

The war artists were all issued cameras to record details of guns, vehicles, buildings, because everything and everyone was in constant flux and it was necessary to be accurate.

In the war pictures it was remarkably useful because you'd get the field sketch and then you'd get a tank at one side but no time to do the details of it, so you'd take a photo. There were many things that happened and then they were over.

Portraiture
According to Comfort, "the successful portrait contains characteristics of both the sitter and the artist. When the mixture is agreeably disposed, the portrait is a work of art."
The agreeable blend of sitter and artist has established Charles Comfort's reputation as one of Canada's finest portrait painters. His first great

"Captain C. F. Comfort, War Artist, Ortona Italy, 1944"

CAPPELLA DI SAN DONATO

In this painting of a ruined Italian chapel, the artist has used light in the Baroque manner, to heighten the sense of dignity, agony and terrible irony of war. The chapel was restored after the war by the Italian government and it stands at the gateway to the Canadian Memorial Cemetery near Ortona.

The Canadian War Museum
The National Museum of Man
National Museums of Canada

14^1/$_2$″ x 21^1/$_2$″   w.c.   War Records 1939-45

CANADIAN 5.5 IN. GUNS

The Canadian War Museum
The National Museum of Man
National Museums of Canada
14³/₈″ x 21¹/₈″   w.c.   War Records 1939-45

BURNING GERMAN MILL
The Canadian War Museum
The National Museum of Man   15¹/₂″ x 22″   w.c.   1939-45

54

155mm. GUNS

Here Comfort uses light in the dramatic, religious 17th century manner. He tended to show the death and destruction of towns and machinery rather than bloodied humans. Because of this, his war paintings have sometimes been criticized as impersonal and unemotional but in his diaries he reveals his feelings. "As they [enemy planes] ended their screaming dive, tracers lacing the sky and black ack-ack bursts surrounding them, bombs started down—only a few hundred feet to fall, [yet] an eternity passes as they slip—silently to their target. All eyes follow—with helpless anguish."

The Canadian War Museum
The National Museum of Man
National Museums of Canada   14¹/₂″ x 21¹/₂″   w.c.   War Records 1939-45

MAJOR W. A. OGILVIE

Comfort's full-face portraits have almost a "signature" in the slight distortion of the left eye. Planned or not, it is indeed effective, for it adds either a diabolic dimension to the character, as in Chuhaldin, or a reflective, somber mood, as in this portrait of his friend Will Ogilvie. The distortion is most apparent in his famous *Young Canadian* where it adds immeasurably to the sense of despair. Several of the portraits of 14th century Giotto, whose work Comfort admires, have a similar fault (or strength), notably the Ognissanti Madonna in Florence.

National Gallery of Canada. Ottawa   33" x 31"   w.c.   1948

56

oil portrait was of his wife Louise, three years after their marriage. Painted against a simple dark background, it has the sparkle of a jewel on velvet. Seven years later in his self-portrait *Portrait in August,* the background of knotted pine boards pushes forward aggressively so that the whole painting seems to be on one plane. In each of his later portraits backdrops of symbolic reference to his sitter close off the space. Three times since 1932 he has painted his artist friend Carl Schaefer as a depression symbol, *Young Canadian,* as *Flight Lieutenant Carl Schaefer,* and finally *Carl Schaefer at Bondhead,* a visionary against a background of rural Ontario. In his portraits of Chuhaldin, *The Violinist,* and Norman Robinson, the *Dreamer,* Comfort intensifies the character of the sitter through his use of symbols. The Chuhaldin is a portrait of the musician and his violin against a richly decorated backdrop. A beautiful recent example of Comfort's use of symbolism is the mystical *New Moon.* It is a landscape with the figure of a nubile girl poised with her back to the viewer facing a new moon. It is sensual and symbolic, this blend of ancient rock, new moon, and young flesh.

Portrait Preparation

To begin, he usually puts on three grounds of white lead, of which the first is applied and then energetically removed with a palette knife. Whereas some artists leave the brush strokes for textural effect, Comfort removes them. The second coat is heavier and smooth.

To Comfort's assertion that in his portraits "the sitter is always there" there have been two exceptions. The first was of a 48th Highlander, a Colonel killed five days before the cease-fire, painted from photographs. The second, and more personally traumatic was his posthumous portrait of his good friend Georges Vanier. This is now the official portrait hanging in Rideau Hall, beside that of another Governor-General, Roland Michener, also painted by Comfort.

Then I do a third over where the head and hands are going to be, if I can guess that. Then I lay an imprimatura . . . a first coat, keyed to the colour and tonality of the painting, e.g. if the painting is going to have a red background then you use a warm imprimatura . . . and not deeper than a middle tone, on the light side. When that is dried I do a charcoal drawing and then it is fixed so that I don't lose it . . . then the outline of the charcoal drawing is done with a warm colour. I might choose vermilion with maybe some light red or some umber in it, or red alone, outlined not heavily but just so that you could paint over it and it could still be seen. Then I wash in the background with a turpentine wash.

From such a seemingly tedious, rational, painterly procedure, many vital or hauntingly heroic portraits have emerged over the years.

PORTRAIT IN AUGUST

The shallow depth of this painting is closed off by a wall of yellow varnished wood. The young artist, front and centre, stares straight at himself and the viewer, no longer tentative, as in *Self-Portrait,* 1921. Here is a tonal drama of light, both direct and reflected, with a sharp feeling of tension between the careful background and the broader treatment of face and shirt.

Collection of Mrs. Charles Comfort   24″ x 30″   oil   1934

THE YOUNG CANADIAN

This water colour of Carl Schaefer is a symbol of the Depression. "I was trying to express the quality of feeling there was for the artist at that time. Both the facial expression and the position of the hands express a feeling of isolation and loneliness, disillusionment and despair."

Hart House, University of Toronto   36" x 42"   w.c.   1932

FL/LT. CARL SCHAEFER

In 1948, when the war was finished, Comfort painted Carl in his airforce uniform, rugged, serious, with the shadow of war still hovering in his eyes.

Art Gallery of Ontario
Gift from the Fund of the T. Eaton Co. Ltd. for Canadian Works of Art, 1948
32³/₈″ x 30³/₈″   w.c.   1948

CARL SCHAEFER AT BOND HEAD

In 1968, at Bond Head, Ontario, Carl Schaefer recalls: "We [Comfort and Schaefer] were up there visiting a doctor friend. We wandered over the fields — I was by the side of the barn with my old oilskin coat on with the largest safety pin I could get to button me up — keep me warm. I was standing alone looking over this vast field of grain." So Comfort sketched him there, and 2 or 3 months later finished the large portrait in bold, broad strokes of colour, delineating the character and independence of his rough-hewn friend.

Collection of L. Bruce Pierce
50" x 67"   oil   1969

CHUHALDIN

This painting is an exciting portrait of Alexander Chuhaldin and his Amati violin. Chuhaldin played his violin at the premiere of Rimsky-Korsakov's Le Coq d'Or and Comfort pictures him against a background stage set for that opera because "it suggested [to me] his flamboyant personality."

Art Gallery of Hamilton
Gift of the Women's Committee, 1954   36" x 42"   w.c.   1931

62

NEW MOON
This remarkable and symbolic painting contrasts the hard, cold, primeval rock, set against the warm, soft, nubile body of a young girl, adding a delicate tracery of light and symbolism with a sliver of moon.

Collection of Dr. Steven Demeter   30" x 60"   oil   1969

War Paintings

During World War I artists were not required to enlist, nor were they sent overseas. They stayed in Canada and painted large canvases which were to be finally hung in a projected memorial building in Ottawa (which was never built). In his book *Artist at War*, Comfort speaks of the preliminary reconnaissance necessary in World War II before commencing a field sketch on the front lines since there were booby traps and mines to avoid. His equipment, of necessity, was easily portable, a collapsible easel which could be set up among the rubble, a small metal stool, watercolour paper 15" × 21". His most poignant paintings are not his war portraits which tend to lack psychological impact, but those crying the havoc of war — the stark silhouette of a bombed building, a silenced mortar, a destroyed Italian village with its sad ruins and a distant figure. The best of these paintings are as gaunt and monumental as those of Giotto whom he admires. In others, his urge for exhaustive detail blunts the impact but it was his job to record the war with an objective and accurate eye.

Oil Painting

Of all his painting, Comfort's landscapes in oil seem to contain the essence of his artistic power. Portraits are restricted by the expectation of the patron, but landscapes are nature interpreted freely by the artist. It is here that Comfort's sensual qualities are most evident. He paints as a gourmet dines — with fastidious and careful selectiveness. He does not flail about with his paintbrush, making angry or absurd statements. It has been his camping trips to Georgian Bay, to the Maritimes, to Haliburton and to the mountains which have given him the greatest pleasure and purest painting. Here his statement about inexhaustible beauty of Nature takes on fire and meaning. To look at his large painting *Tadoussac*, 1935, as one critic did, and see only the geometry of his houses and the juxtaposition of straight and curved line in careful composition, is to miss the point of Charles Comfort's painting. It stirs the senses as no modern hard-edge painting could do. The elimination of all but the barest of forms here adopts the ideas but not the execution of Piet Mondrian. The impact remains sensual.

How does Comfort decide which of many sketches done on a camping trip he will make into a large painting? In his words, "Many of my major works are a combination of several field sketches." He searches for composition and mood. His assertion, "I am very interested in mood" comes as no surprise and he employs rich, mellow colour to achieve this mood. Only occasionally does the search for mood lead him into an excess of strong blue or deep red, reducing and overwhelming the basic form and line. He will sometimes return to a painting in his possession from time to time for further work. "One always feels a painting should have something further done to it." On commissions

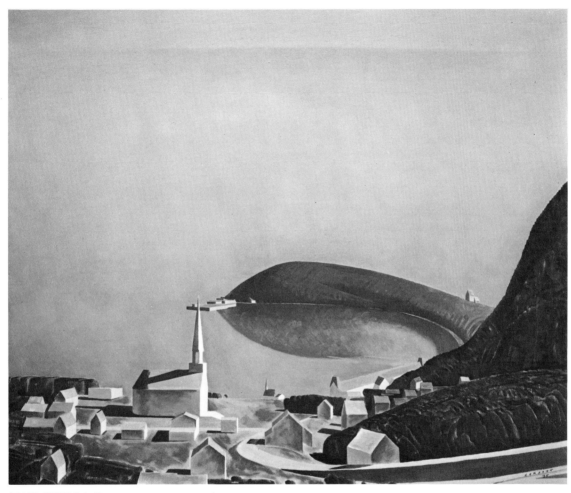

TADOUSSAC

The impact of Katherine Dreier's contemporary 1927 art show in Toronto probably influenced Comfort who began to simplify his painting. In *Tadoussac*, the reduction resulted in a painting of great atmospheric beauty. It is not enough to comment as one critic did that the houses are boxlike and the land a series of arcs. Comfort places the viewer high above the scene, leaving two-thirds of the canvas almost blank, a calm vista enveloped in faint mist, finally thrusting a promontory in a great swoop out into the sea. Some of the spell is lost in black and white but the painting remains a breathless setting for an ancient "faerie" tale.

The National Gallery of Canada, Ottawa
Bequest of Vincent Massey, 1968   30" x 36"   oil   1935

"Charles Comfort in his studio, 1975"

THRUSH SONG

This rare abstract exhibits the artist's sensitivity to colour and structure — his unerring sense of design. The artist comments, "I began to experiment with Abstract Expressionism following the impact of the exhibition of the Société Anonyme in the Art Gallery of Toronto in 1927. It has been a sporadic parallel [throughout his painting career]."

Collection of the Artist
26″ x 20″   mixed media   1948

ISLE OF MULL
This Scottish landscape is a monumental painting, realistic, serene, perhaps lacking in the romantic vision with which Comfort often infused his Canadian scenes, but his sense of colour is exquisite.

Collection of Mr. & Mrs. L. H. Marsland   20" x 26"   oil   1971

EDGE OF THE WORLD

Time and again we are made aware of Comfort's superb sense of colour, harmony and tone — there is unerring beauty, even a voluptuous quality to his best landscapes, especially in the flesh tones of the Georgian Bay rocks. This is a view of the outer islands beyond the northern entrance to Monument Channel in Georgian Bay.

Private Collection   12" x 16"   oil   1972

TURBULENT SEAS Ingonish, Cape Breton
In recent years the Comforts have turned away from the rugged Georgian Bay to the less physically demanding Cape Breton for the annual sketching trip. In his seventies, Charles Comfort is still in thrall to the romanticism and challenge of nature.

Private Collection   12″ x 16″   oil on board   1973

HARBOUR Ingonish, Oliver's Boat

For the past three summers in Cape Breton Comfort has painted the sea in its many moods. Here is a sunny array of fishing boats in a quiet harbour with mountain and cloud shapes of the background echoing the shapes of the shore and boat in the foreground.

Collection of Dr. Steven Demeter   12" x 16"   oil   1974

he works to a schedule, but otherwise he enjoys a flexible daily routine, working usually on three paintings at once in his studio, a somewhat cluttered, exciting place dominated by a large, ancient easel.

Palette
On sketching trips Comfort used to work 10" × 12" panels, but now he works in a size to fit his box, 12" × 16".

I carry three panels. That would be a big day's work, but I often do two in a day. I make my drawing, then outline the pencil usually with Alizarin crimson.

From left to right his palette reads:

Naples yellow, yellow ochre, raw sienna, raw umber, burnt umber . . . both Alizarin crimson and either vermilion or scarlet vermilion, two blues, cobalt and cerulean . . . then veridian. That would be how I'd set my palette but I have extra colours in my box for accents, cobalt violet, or maybe bright cadmium. I use Winsor & Newton paints—always have done.

Like many artists he is having difficulty getting both paint and canvas these days.

I always use flake white #2, a sort of medium consistency. Of course I have black on my palette

— I never use it but you never can tell. For medium? A mixture of linseed oil with a little turpentine, a dash of drier. When I say a dash I mean I stick the end of a match into a bottle of drier and stir it into my medium . . . less than a drop. It helps the surface dry a little more quickly . . . important when you're travelling.

Comfort and Jackson
Comfort often painted in Georgian Bay with his old friend A. Y. Jackson.

The moment we got there he [Jackson] would say: "Well, I'm going to sit down here," and first thing I knew he had his box out, a very small box —he did small paintings. He'd whip out a brush and put some raw sienna on the palette and start right in. He never bothered with charcoal, or pencil . . . [Then, after a long pause] But I don't like the sun shining on the surface that I'm going to paint. I take a stool, an umbrella. It takes me maybe fifteen minutes to get set up. Alec didn't bother with that. He sat on the ground or on a rock. He'd done it all his life and was hardened to it. I've always wanted to enjoy some comfortable support. And then I'd set my palette, and I always made the drawing on my small panels with pencil.

The Abstract Experiment

Charles Comfort's sophisticated realistic style is as different from abstract painting as freedom is from licence. He would not agree with Wyndham Lewis that "the art instinct is permanently primitive." He considers great globs of paint untidy and obscuring and avoids building up texture for dramatic effect. But whereas his own work has been that of a rational craftsman, as a teacher and later as Director of the National Gallery, Comfort brought to these posts his characteristic understanding and tolerance of the modern experiments. Over the years he has privately and steadily experimented with abstract art, mainly in acrylic, building up a small but impressive body of abstract works. They reflect his admiration for Piet Mondrian's "Organic Geometrical" painting. His nature rejects the disorderly and emotional qualities of the abstract expressionists. "I don't like confused manifestations, like action painting and the automatistes . . . They are just trying to destroy the past." So, although he derives pleasure from pure linear abstraction, it could never satisfy Comfort completely and has remained a sporadic parallel to his "real" painting.

Heritage

Charles Comfort speaks of painters whom he admired in his formative years and it is from three of these in particular that we catch flickers of response in his own work. The influence of Geertgen tot Sint Jans, a Dutch fifteenth-century artist noted for his precocious use of light can be seen in the diffused radiance of Comfort's smooth textural paintings.

Comfort admired the simplicity and craftsmanship of Giotto, the fourteenth-century genius, which is reflected in the monumentality and reduction of form in the many murals which Comfort painted. He responded ultimately to the warmth of the curved rather than the geometric line.

Piet Mondrian, Dutch abstractionist of the twentieth century may have moved Comfort toward his very strong sensitivity for balance and composition, not only in his abstracts, but in all his work.

Though he may make his own images out of his own time and experience, yet the artist must acknowledge his inheritance and these three painters may well have subtly enriched the work of Charles Comfort, twentieth-century Canadian.

Chronology

Charles Fraser Comfort, Born 22 July, 1900, at Cramond, near Edinburgh, Scotland.

1912 – Came to Canada with his family, settled in Winnipeg, Man.

1913 – Began work at Bridgen's Studio, Winnipeg.

1915 – Attended Kevin Technical School in the evenings.

1916 – Attended Winnipeg School of Art in the evenings.

1920 – Joined Arts & Letters Club, Toronto.

1922 – Exhibition, Winnipeg Art Gallery.

1922-1923 – Attended Art Students' League in New York.

1924 – Returned to Winnipeg. Married Louise Irene Chase.

1925 – Moved to Toronto to work at Brigden's Toronto Studio.

1926 – Became member of Canadian Society of Painters in Water Colour (later president).

1927 – Became member of Ontario Society of Artists; received Honourable Mention in Willingdon Art Competition for portrait *Louise*; elder daughter born.

1929 – Employed by Rapid, Grip & Batten, Ltd. for two years; younger daughter born.

1931 – Established commercial studio with William Ogilvie and Harold Ayres.

1933 – Founding member, Canadian Group of Painters (later president).

1935-1938 – Taught at Ontario College of Art.

1938 – Joined Faculty of Department of Art and Archeology, University of Toronto; first award, Great Lakes Exhibition.

1939 – Joined Canadian Officers Training Corps, commissioned and made Infantry Rifle Instructor.

1942 – Associate, Royal Canadian Academy (later, Academician).

1943-1946 – Senior War Artist, Royal Canadian Armed Forces.

1945 – Designed the Canadian Volunteer Service Medal.

1946-1960 – Associate Professor, Department of Fine Art, University of Toronto.

1951 – First Award, Ontario Society of Artists.

1955 – Awarded Royal Society Fellowship, studied in the Netherlands.

1958 – Honourary Degree, Mount Allison University.

1959 – Delegate, NATO Conference, London, England.

1960-1965 – Director, National Gallery of Canada.

1963 – Awarded Gold Medal, University of Alberta; awarded Medaglio al Merito Culturale, Republic of Italy.

1967 – Awarded Centennial Medal.

1972 – Officer of the Order of Canada.

Selected Bibliography

Boggs, Jean Sutherland, *The National Gallery of Canada*, London: Thames & Hudson, 1971.

Buchanan, Donald W., *The Growth of Canadian Painting*, London: Collins, 1958.

Canadian Paintings in Hart House, J. Russell Harper ed., Toronto: University of Toronto Press, 1955.

Colgate, William, *Canadian Art, Its Origin and Development*, Toronto: Ryerson Press, 1945.

Comfort, Charles, *The Painter and His Model*, Open House, W. A. Beacon and Wilfred Reeves, eds., Ottawa: Graphic Publishers, Ltd., 1931.

Duval, Paul, *Canadian Watercolor Painting*. Toronto: Burns & MacEachern, 1954.

Harper, J. Russell, *Painting in Canada*, Toronto: University of Toronto Press, 1966.

Hubbard, R. H., The Development of Canadian Art, Ottawa: Queen's Printer, 1963.

MacDonald, Colin A., *A Dictionary of Canadian Artists*, Vol. 1, Ottawa: 1967, p. 139-142.

Middleton, Jesse, *Canadian Landscape*; as pictured by F. H. Brigden, Toronto: Ryerson Press, 1944, p. 111.

Reid, Dennis, *A Concise History of Canadian Painting*, Toronto: Oxford University Press, 1973.

Yearbook of the Arts in Canada, Bertram Brooker, ed., Toronto: The Macmillan Company of Canada, 1928-9, p. 234-5.

Also exhibition catalogues and newspaper and magazine articles.

Books and Articles by Charles Comfort:

Artist at War, Toronto: Ryerson Press, October, 1956.

Journey 1924-64, Privately Printed, 1964.

The Moro River and Other Observations, Privately Printed, 1970.

Paintings: An Essay Prepared for the Royal Commission on National Development in the Arts, Letters and Sciences, 1949-1951. Ottawa, 1951.

Tempus Fugit, Privately Printed, 1962.

Printed and Bound in Hong Kong